AF882390

Table of Contents

Part One – Hit the Ground Running

At a young age, sometimes we work and hustle to maintain the things we want. Once we hit adulthood, most adults work long draining hours just to maintain the things we need. This is because many of those adults have been thrown into the world without the most important tools for success. Well, I am here to help you understand everything they don't teach us in school. Using these tools will give you the opportunity to hit the ground running once you enter adulthood.

Goals and Objectives

If you want to hit the ground running, the easiest way to transition into adulthood is with a plan. Goals and objectives are basically just the dreams that we're sleeping on. So, wake up, write them down and put them into action.

Where do you see yourself ONE year from now?

Age?

Career Goals?

Educational Goals?

Social Goals?

Where do you see yourself FIVE years from now?

Age?

Career Goals?

Educational Goals?

Social Goals?

Now take the goals from each part of your life [one year, five years and ten years] and write them out in the circles as your end result. Then use the boxes to write down your objectives – or the steppingstones for how you plan to reach each goal.

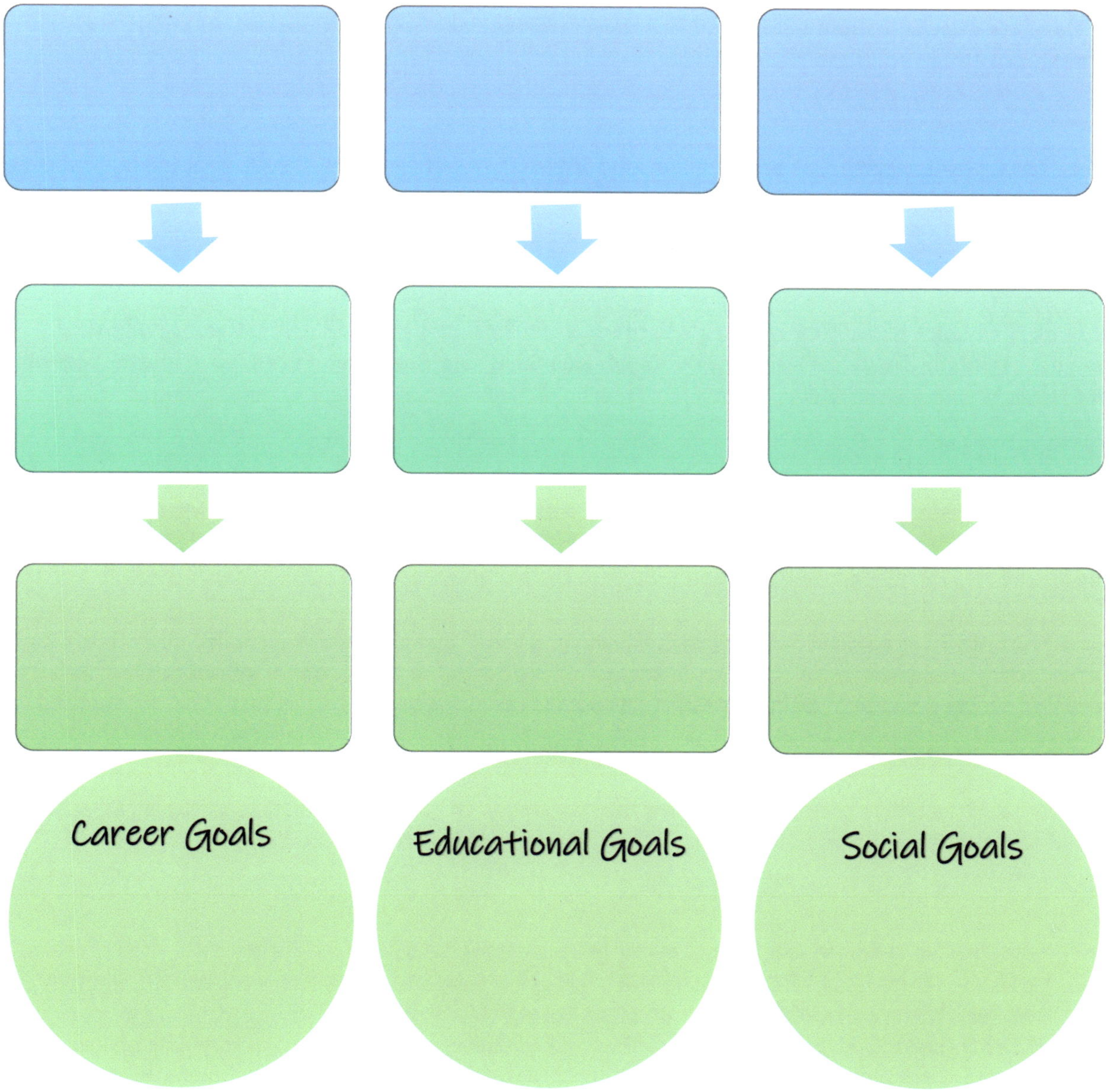

Resume Writing

Building a resume is much easier than it seems. It is simply a marketing Ad about you to the company you're applying for. Follow the steps below to tailor the perfect resume for the next job you're seeking.

Heading.

Your heading should include your basic contact information – Name, Contact Number, Email Address, and Home Address

Objective.

Think about the position you are seeking and identify what you are trying to pursue. You also want to identify what you have to offer in the field you are applying. Your objective should be about two short sentences.

Education.

Simply outline your education history starting with the most recent school you graduated from or attended. Include the school's name, address, the time you attended and any degrees or certificate you've earned.

Work Experience.

Outline the jobs you've had over the years and include: the name of the company, the years you worked there, the position you held and your job description. Also include any awards or special honors you received on the job.

Skills.

Chose a few skills that go hand and hand with whatever job you're applying for and specific skills that'll help you stand out. For example, using skills like "Microsoft Office Savvy" or "Proficient in Microsoft Excel" is better than simply stating you have "Computer Skills" on your resume.

References.

List a few people you have professional working relationships with and their contact information. Of course, you want your references to be people that will have the best things to say about you.

Tips

- You should be updating your resume every time you apply for a job in a different field – fast food, retail, call centers, etc. all require different skills, objectives and sometimes work history. However, your work history should always be the same and show consistency.
- ALWAYS ALWAYS ALWAYS check for spelling and grammar errors. Certain parts of the resume don't require full sentences but one of the most important details [some] employers look for is spelling and grammar errors.
- Keep your contact information up to date and make sure your email is professional.

There is an example on the next page of what your resume should look like once it is put together.

Jane Doe

123 South St
Franklin, MI

(313) 555 – 5050

janedoe@email.com

Objective

To secure a long-term position with opportunities for growth to expand my knowledge and skills in my field

Education

South State University – Sunnyside, CA

- Bachelor of Science in Business Administration – 2019

South City High School – Franklin, MI

- Class of 2014

Experience

March 2018 – Present
Administrative Assistant • Global Health Services

- Manage and distribute information within the office. Answered phones, maintained files, and organized and scheduled appointments

January 2016 – November 2017
Waitress • Lucy's Bar and Grill

- Provided exceptional service to all customers ensuring that everyone I serviced left satisfied
- Employee of the Month April 2017 and July 2017

June 2014 – August 2014
Camp Counselor • Springhill Summer Camp

- Responsible for the overall supervision of campers and providing them with an enjoyable experience

Skills

- Proficient in all Microsoft Office Programs
- Accounting and Bookkeeping; Skilled in QuickBooks software
- Editing Skills, Strong Attention to Detail

References

- John Smith – Office Manager – Global Health Services

  Contact: (313)555 – 5555 and johnsmith@email.com

Interview Tips

A lot of people dread interviews because there are those few questions that they have no idea how to answer. I have outlined a few of the toughest interview questions and the best way to answer them. However, no matter how much advice you get before an interview, doing research on the company ahead of time will always place you a few steps ahead.

1. What are your strengths and weaknesses?

   It's easy for us to name our strengths, but weaknesses aren't hard to acknowledge either, if you're prepared. If you know what's expected of the employees, name a weakness that has absolutely nothing to do with the job description. Make your weakness work in your favor

   Examples: Call Center – Not good at standing long hours

   Warehouse/Factory – Not good with public speaking

   Childcare – Don't work well with being micromanaged, prefer to take leadership on tasks

   Data Entry – Extremely detailed, tend to over analyze things

2. Name a problem you solved or an obstacle you overcame.

   This question is not about the problem, the interviewer is inquiring about your resolution skills. So, whatever problem you use as an example, make sure it's a time you showed your best ethical judgment.

3. Why should we hire you?

   In other words, what can you do for us? Advise the interviewer what you can bring to the table. Be sure your assets align with what is expected of the employees.

4. Why do you want to work here?

   You don't want to say something as simple as pay or just stating how desperately you need a job. This is where the research really becomes useful. When you're looking up a company, outline a few things you like best and use those points for why you want to work with the company.

5. What critical feedback do you receive often?

   Like your weakness, discuss feedback that you've received that doesn't interfere with the job description. Whether the feedback has come from an employee, teacher, friend or family member, aim for something that you have been improving on as well.

Part Two – Let the Bag Chase You

When you want something to grow or last for a long time, your first thought should be a solid foundation. This is true for plants, building a home, and even building finances. The goal for finance is not how fast you can add up your money, it is a solid foundation so that every seed you plant is guaranteed to grow a fruitful outcome.

Financial Institutions

This section will allow you to weigh your banking options. It outlines details to help you chose the best financial institution to start building a solid financial foundation.

Bank	Credit Union
For Profit	Not for Profit
Deposit insurance provided by FDIC – Federal Deposit Insurance Corporation	Deposit insurance provided by NCUA – National Credit Union Administration
Offers more diverse products	Financial products may be limited
Anyone can apply for an account	Must qualify for membership to open account
Owned by shareholders and run by business owners	Owned by members and governed by a board of directors

Checking	Savings
Easy and immediate access to money	Designed for long term savings
Debit cards used for direct withdrawal	Limited number of withdrawals per month (6) Regulation D is a federal law that prohibits more than 6 withdrawals per month in order to help banks maintain reserve requirements
Money withdrawn through bank or ATM	Most banks don't let you withdraw money from your savings at the ATM. However, you can withdraw funds directly from the bank, an internal transfer from savings to checking, or a wire transfer.
Offers low interest rates on high deposits	Offers higher interest rates than checking accounts and most don't require a minimum deposit to collect interest
Checking and savings accounts can be easily linked to make deposits, withdrawals and transfers.	

Budgeting

I know that it may seem pointless, like "I can just budget everything in my head". However, we all hate the moments where we turn and wonder what happened to the $20 or $50 that disappeared. Nobody stole it, you didn't lose it, you just forgot how you spent it. Budgeting helps you avoid wondering how you lost $275 going out, when you were only supposed to spend $150.

Here is a simple sample of a budget and an example on how to use it:

Weekly Budget Example			
Description	Income (+)	Expense (-)	$ Available
Earnings (Hair Clients)	$650		$650
Savings		$300	$350
Entertainment		$100	$250
Food		$150	$100
Transportation (Lyft)		$100	$0
Total	**$650**	**$650**	**$0**

Be sure that your budget is balanced on both sides. If your total income doesn't match your total expenses, then there is money that you haven't accounted for.

Weekly Budget Example			
Description	Income (+)	Expense (-)	$ Available

Weekly Budget Example			
Description	Income (+)	Expense (-)	$ Available

Weekly Budget Example			
Description	Income (+)	Expense (-)	$ Available

Credit Building

Your credit score is a rating finance companies use to determine how trustworthy you are with borrowing money. This section will explain everything you need to know about credit and how to get started on building your score.

Credit Advantages	Credit Disadvantages
Making immediate purchase with anticipated income (should be for emergencies only)	Interest charged on payments
Making large purchase and paying in small portions	Overspending [resulting in] financial trouble

Credit Bureaus or CRA (Credit Reporting Agencies) collect and maintain consumer credit information to build consumer credit reports. The three Bureaus are:

1. Equifax
2. Experian
3. Transunion

Credit Reports are statements about your credit activity over time including personal information, registered addresses, loan and credit card payment history and much more.

Type of Credit	Example
Installment Credit **is debt repaid on a fixed schedule**	Auto Loans, Student Loans, or Mortgage Loans
Revolving Credit **does not have a fixed number of payments**	Credit Cards, Retail Cards, and personal lines of credit

How to Start Building Credit?

1. Become an authorized user on someone's credit card. This will benefit your credit history length, which is difficult to build on and doesn't change often at all.
2. Get a secured credit card or loan. Secured cards and loans are a little easier to get than most credit accounts, but they require a deposit. Unsecured cards and loans are given without a deposit but requires a certain credit score and/or collateral.

Secured Credit Cards to get you started:	
Discover It	$0 Annual Fee – 22.99% Variable APR – 300-629 Credit Score Required
Open Sky Visa	$35 Annual Fee – 17.39% Variable APR – 300-689 Credit Score Required
Greendot Visa	$49 Annual Fee – 9.99% Variable APR – 300-850 Credit Score Required
Capital One (Secured)	$0 Annual Fee – 26.99% Variable APR – 300

Variable APR is the annual percentage rate of interest you pay for borrowing money [per year]. "Variable" means your interest rate can change over time. You can avoid interest rates by paying accounts off before the end of the billing cycle.

How is interest calculated?

- First, use your APR (26.99%) and divide by 365 (days in the year) to calculate the daily interest rate. Which, in this case, would be $0.074
- Next, you'll multiply your balance for the month ($300) times the daily interest rate ($0.074) $300 x $0.074 = $22.18
- So, the interest you would be paying for the month is $22.18 on top of your $300 balance.

Score Fluctuations – How does your score change?		
Credit Factor	Increase	Decrease
Payment History	Early/Ontime Payment	Late/Missed Payments
Credit Utilization	Low Credit Balance	High Credit Balance
Credit Utilization	High Amounts of Available Credit	Low Amounts of Available Credit
Derogatory Marks	Avoid Collections Accounts	Credit account sent to debt collector
Age of Credit History	Long Credit History Length	Little to no credit history
Total Accounts	10+ accounts including closed and paid off accounts over time. Take your time when building your total accounts to avoid too many credit inquiries.	Less than 5 total credit accounts will typically show little to no credit history.
Hard Inquiries	Avoid submitting too many credit applications (try to limit 2 per year) Inquiries will fall off your report every two years.	Submitting too many credit applications in a year will have a negative impact on your credit score

The **Number ONE Rule** with credit is

DO NOT run up more debt than you can afford to PAY BACK!

Forgetting this rule is what causes people to dig themselves in a hole of debt that is hard to get out of.

Part Three – Hustle Hard

Life is about choices, and whether you choose to be led or lead others, make the choice to get started somewhere. If you're one of those people that can't imagine being stuck under someone else's management, consider starting a business you can manage on your own.

This section will outline everything you need to know about developing a business plan and the steps you need to take in order to put that plan into action.

Creating a Plan

Starting a business is simple. The hardest part about being a business owner is managing and expanding your opportunities and assets. The planning process is the easiest part. Once you walk through these simple questions, you'll have a full business plan prepared.

1. **(Description) Who** will be doing business? Will there be partners or co-owners involved? List the name of your company and anyone that will have ownership of the business. List the personal information for yourself and everyone on your team.

2. **(Description Continued) What** type of business are you building? Describe the goods and/or services you will offer. Also consider the legal structure of your business entity – sole proprietorship, partnership, LLC, corporation, etc. (See page 21 to help you determine this). Where will you be doing business? Online or a storefront?

3. **(Startup Goals) When** do you plan to start executing your business plan? Establish a start date, then a list of things you will need to do to get started. Create a deadline for everything on your list as well. This will help you track your progress and keep you on track with getting your goals done.

4. **(Mission Statement) Why** will you do business? What is your purpose for starting a business? Explain the purpose and values of your business in a few short sentences.

5. **(Budgeting and Financing) How** will you fund your business? Outline sources to fund your investment, then create a budget.

Write down all your expenses, how much you need and how much each item costs. Then, multiply your quantity by your cost per item to get the total cost.

Budget

Expense	Quantity	Cost Per Item	Total Costs

Estimated Earnings

Good and/or Services	Selling Cost x (Quantity)	Total Earnings
Calculating Profit		
Total Earnings	Total Startup Costs	Total Profit

Simple way to calculate your Profit:

Revenue (Total Earnings) – Total Cost/Expenses = Total Profit

The Next Steps

First, make sure you research everything! Being as knowledgeable as possible is what will keep you motivated and limit most of the doubts you might have. With this entire handbook you should use additional resources to go in depth about everything you want to educate yourself on.

Funding

Once your business plan is complete, the hardest factor in the process of being self-employed is funding your dream. Depending on the nature of your business, you can always start small, save and fund your dream out of pocket. However, for those bigger dreams that may need a lump sum of cash for startup, here are a few **Funding Resources:**

- Gofundme.com is commonly known for a wide variety of uses but this crowd funding website is perfect to raise funds for new businesses. Use the website or app to share your fund-raising post and get support from family, friends and even strangers.
- Prosperusdetroit.org has several links for funding resources including lenders, crowdfunding and assistance with funding.
- Secured Credit Cards (or Unsecured Credit Cards) can be used to fund large business expenses and paid off overtime. This will also help you build business credit for larger payments as your business grows.

Legal Structure

Now that you know how you'll pay for your business, it's time to solidify the foundation. The chart below will help you choose the right business structure. Your business structure will help you determine legal and tax considerations, so you will have a better idea of the next steps you will need to take regarding registering your business and obtaining tax ID numbers.

Common Business Structures–Pros and Cons

Business Structure	What is it?	Advantages	Disadvantages
Sole Proprietorship	An enterprise owned and run by One person	1. Not much required to set up 2. Direct control 3. Low startup costs	1. Difficult to raise capital 2. Owner personally liable for all debts and obligations
Partnership	An enterprise owned and run by more than one person	1. Tax Advantages 2. More partners, more funds 3. Easy to form	1. Owners are personally liable 2. Joint accountability amongst all owners 3. Difference of opinion and slower decision making
LLC (Limited Liability Corporation)	A hybrid entity that is easy to establish like a sole proprietorship/partnership but shares the benefits of a corporation	1. Easy to form 2. Tax Flexibility 3. Personal Liability Protection 4. No limit on number of Members	1. Taxes and Fees 2. Higher Legal Expenses 3. Limited Transferability of Ownership 4. Formalities and Reporting Requirements – Article of Organization
Corporation	A business entity, usually owned by a group of people, that acts as a single entity	1. Personal Liability Protection 2. Ability to sell stock increasing chances of earning financial capital 3. Established structure with defined roles and accountabilities	1. Time Consuming, Expensive and lots of paperwork needs to be filed 2. Regulations leave little room for flexibility 3. Possibility of double taxation – profits and dividends paid to stockholders are taxed

After deciding on which business structure you will be using, you can file all the necessary paperwork on legalzoom.com. Legal Zoom is a legal technology company that processes files for various reasons but mainly known for their easy and helpful process for filing new businesses. They offer legal advice and any additional legal essentials you may need to run your business. Pricing packages vary depending on the business structure and state.

Understanding the Risks! The world today may make it seem as if quitting a nine to five and being your own boss is what we should ALL be doing. However, before you jump into starting a business you need to know some of the most common risks.

1. **Financial Risks and Bankruptcy.** With all the money you spend on your business, it takes some time to rebuild your earnings and turn them into actual profits. Imagine a kid spending $50 to start a lemonade stand – the kid won't actually make any money (profit) until after earning the $50 they spent to get started. The larger your business is, the longer it may take to earn a profit. Budget and manage your expenses properly to avoid putting all of your personal assets into your dreams and possibly going into debt.
2. **Competitive Risks.** In business, you will be competing with other companies in your target market. If there are a lot of hairstylists and barbers in your area, you're going to have to work harder to get customers coming in and coming back, especially if you're new in business. Before starting a business, you should always research to know how competitive the market you're entering will be. You also want to know who your competitors are and what they offer to help your products and services stand out.
3. **Legal Liability Risks.** When you face a legal issue, your business – and in some cases, your personal assets – can be at risk. This is why it is important to know and understand the laws and regulations in the state you'll be doing business in.
4. **Economic Risks.** No one has the power to predict every time a recession will occur, but economic downturns are inevitable. Like we've seen with the COVID-19 pandemic, changes in government regulations can have a huge impact on businesses regardless of how big or small they are. The entertainment industry – a market that isn't affected nearly as often as most other businesses – was even heavily impacted during the pandemic due to social distancing requirements.

A risk doesn't result in a sure failure, it just brings awareness to the possibilities for setbacks. So, know what you're getting yourself into and build a solid plan to overcome any obstacles you might face.

Useful Terms

- **Accounting** – the action or process of keeping financial accounts
- **Accounts Receivable** – money owed to a company by its debtors
- **Accounts Payable** – money owed by a company to its creditors
- **Assets** – resources owned by a company with economic value including cash, inventory, land, etc.
- **Balance Sheet** – a statement of the assets, liabilities, and capital of a business detailing the balance of income and expenses over time
- **Budget** – an estimate of income and expenses over time
- **Capital** – money needed to produce goods and services
- **Cash Flow** – the total amount of money being transferred into and out of a business
- **Depreciation** – the decrease of value in an asset over time due to wear and tear
- **Dividends** – the cash corporations pay to stockholders
- **Expense** – the cost of operations that a company acquires to generate revenue
- **Fiscal Year** – one-year period that businesses and governments use for financial budgeting and reporting
- **Liabilities** – obligations or debts a person or company owes
- **Market Value** – estimated value of an asset based on how much a buyer would be willing to pay the seller
- **Net Loss** – when expenses exceed the income or total revenue for a given period of time
- **Net Profit** – the profit of a company after operating expenses and all other charges including taxes, interest and depreciation have been deducted from total revenue
- **Owner's Equity** – what's left over for the owner after you've subtracted all the liabilities from the assets
- **Profit Margin** – a ratio of a company's profit (sales minus all expenses) divided by its revenue
- **Profit and Loss Statement** – a financial statement that summarizes the revenues, costs, and expenses incurred during a specified period, usually a fiscal quarter or year
- **Revenue** – the total amount of income generated by the sale of goods or services
- **Working Capital** – the amount of available capital that a company can readily use for day-to-day operations

Made in the USA
Las Vegas, NV
03 November 2026

57424183R00017